TRANSFORMING
STIGMA
WORKBOOK

HOW TO BECOME A
MENTAL WELLNESS
SUPERHERO

Published by Mike Veny, Inc.
First edition.
ISBN: 978-0-578-49524-8

Cover design by Ida Fia Sveningsson (www.idafiasveningsson.se) and Streetlight Graphics (www.streetlightgraphics.com)
Formatting by Streetlight Graphics (www.streetlightgraphics.com)
Editing by Katie Chambers (beaconpointservices.org) and Christie Stratos, Proof Positive (www.proofpositivepro.com)
Proofreading by Kate Tilton (www.katetilton.com)

DEDICATION

This book is dedicated to Dana McCrary. Thank you for letting me know that you needed a more effective way of applying the material from my first book. Thank you for your honest conversations with me. Thank you for all that you do for youth and families.

DISCLAIMER

Trigger Warning: This book discusses violence, self-harm, and suicide.

If you or someone you know may be struggling with suicidal thoughts, you can call the **U.S. National Suicide Prevention Lifeline** at 800-273-TALK (8255) any time day or night.

Disclaimer: The purpose of this book is to educate and entertain. The author and/or publisher shall have neither liability nor responsibility to anyone with respect to any loss or damaged caused, directly or indirectly, by the information contained in this book. The author is not a mental health professional. If you need medical help, please consult a doctor. **If you are in an emergency, please call 911.**

Author Note: Throughout this book the author uses the term "mental health challenges" in places where one might typically say "mental health issues" or "mental illness". He made the decision to do this because "mental health challenges" feels less stigmatizing to him.

Some names and identifying details have been changed to protect the privacy of individuals.

I hope you find this book to be helpful. If you have any feedback or questions, here's how to contact me:

Mike Veny

PO Box 150252

Kew Gardens, New York 11415-0252

USA

INTRODUCTION

Dear Mental Wellness Superhero in Training,

We face an uphill battle. According to NAMI (National Alliance on Mental Illness), one in five adults in the US experiences mental illness in a given year. Due to the stigma surrounding mental health, most likely even more adults experience it. Millions of undiagnosed and untreated mental illnesses are impacting the lives of incredible people like you, your friends and family, and others. A staggering 90 percent of all those who die by suicide have an underlying mental health challenge, and suicide has risen to the second leading cause of death among ten to thirty-four-year-olds according to NIMH (National Institute of Mental Health).

There *is* a solution to this problem, and you are now an important part of it. I want to thank you and congratulate you for choosing to make a difference. Whether you have read *Transforming Stigma: How to Become a Mental Wellness Superhero* or not, this workbook will help you better understand yourself or a loved one. You can dive into applying this knowledge right now, or you can keep this knowledge on hand for a rainy day. Regardless of how you decide to use it, you have taken the first step toward an impactful and collaborative journey.

As someone who has struggled with mental health challenges my entire life, I have now dedicated my existence to helping those who struggle, and I am humbled to guide you on this journey. It will not be easy, but it will be powerful, as our destination is a place where those with mental health challenges are supported, violent tragedies are prevented, and suicides are no longer claiming the lives of our friends, family, and neighbors.

I created this workbook to empower you. You can escape being a spectator on the sidelines and instead be the mental wellness superhero you or someone you love needs. After completing this workbook, you will have a deeper understanding and the ability to use effective tools to transform stigma. You will gain powers that you didn't even know existed. It's time to change the world. People—maybe even yourself or a loved one—need your help. Will you answer their call?

Your superhero training begins today!
Earn your cape by completing this workbook!

Sincerely,

Mike Veny

PREPARE YOURSELF

A S YOU'RE PREPARING TO BECOME a mental wellness superhero, you will want to get the most out of this workbook by following these five recommendations:

1. You do not have to read *Transforming Stigma: How to Become a Mental Wellness Superhero* in order to benefit from this workbook. However, reading the book will give you a fuller view of each topic and additional tips on self-care and insight into stigma and the Stigma Cycle.

2. Allow your written responses or conversations in a group discussion to go whatever direction they choose. Use the space provided for your responses or use your favorite journal.

3. Start anywhere in the workbook. Although the sections and questions are structured in a way that I feel will be the most beneficial, do not feel bound to go in order from section to section.

4. If you are using this workbook to guide you in your journaling, free yourself from distractions and complete sections of the workbook in a space you're comfortable in. Consider putting your phone on silent, closing out your email inbox, and putting on some calming music.

5. Schedule more time than you feel is needed to complete each section.

GROUP DISCUSSIONS

The following sections and questions were crafted to help facilitate self-reflection and learning and to be perfect discussion questions for groups. For group discussions, I recommend group members complete the sections individually first, completing only one section at a time, and then meet back as a group to discuss each member's individual responses.

At the end of each group meeting, I highly recommend the facilitator ask these three questions:

1. What question was the hardest for you to answer and why?

2. If you could add one question to this section that you would like to answer, what would you add and why?

3. What questions would you ask the author about this topic?

UNDERSTANDING STIGMA

OVERVIEW

I N CHAPTER SEVEN OF *TRANSFORMING Stigma*, I give the definitions of stigma and its various facets from Merriam-Webster.

Stigma: *"A set of negative and often unfair beliefs that a society or group of people have about something."*

Stigma typically includes:

1. Stereotypes: "To believe unfairly that all people or things with a particular characteristic are the same."

   Example: Everyone with Obsessive Compulsive Disorder washes their hands repeatedly.

2. Prejudice: "A feeling of like or dislike for someone or something especially when it is not reasonable or logical."

   Example: I just don't like to be around people who have a mental health challenge.

3. Discrimination: "The practice of unfairly treating a person or group of people differently from other people or groups of people."

   Example: They can't come on this trip with us since they have ADHD. They might ruin the fun for the rest of us.

In essence, stereotypes are related to thoughts, prejudice comes from feelings, and discrimination relates to a person's behavior. Stigma, like mental health, impacts our thoughts, feelings, and behaviors.

UNDERSTANDING STIGMA EXERCISE

How has the stigma surrounding mental health played out in your life? If you have not experienced it, why do you think that is?

_____

_____

_____

_____

How could the following aspects of stigma affect someone who has a mental health challenge? Refer back to the overview of this section for definitions of each.

Stereotypes:

_____

_____

_____

_____

Prejudice:

_____

_____

_____

_____

Discrimination:

_____

_____

_____

_____

In what ways could stigma impact a person overall who has a mental health challenge? (Check all that apply.)

☐ Lower self-confidence

☐ Bring about depression

☐ Lead to self-destructive behaviors

☐ Provoke to isolate from others

☐ Discourage discussing it

☐ Forgo or avoid medication

☐ Refuse to start or continue care

☐ Trigger a panic attack

☐ Worsen their mental health condition

Remembering all three aspects of stigma, what actions could you take to stop hurtful stereotypes, prejudice, and discrimination affecting those with real or perceived mental health challenges?

_____

_____

_____

_____

In what ways could companies, organizations, and groups of people stop hurtful stereotypes, prejudice, and discrimination affecting those with mental health challenges?

_____

_____

_____

_____

Scenario:

Drew suffers from a mental health challenge. Drew took several days off work and is trying to explain to their boss why they needed this time off. They worry if they share this challenge with their employer, they may be fired, not treated the same as others, or not given equal opportunities to move up the company ladder in the future.

As Drew's friend, what advice would you give them?

_____

_____

_____

_____

WHAT STIGMA LOOKS LIKE EXERCISE

You now have a better understanding of what stigma is, but I would like you to now explore this understanding and what it means to you. Take a few minutes to complete the following exercises.

#1. In your own words, define what stigma is without looking up a definition or revisiting the section above.

Stigma is: _____

_____

#2. Draw what stigma looks like as a person below.

#3. Now describe stigma, the person, as you have drawn them above.

_____

_____

_____

_____

_____

#4. Share your definition and picture with your group. I would also love to hear your definition, see your picture, and read your description of stigma. Post on social media, tag @MikeVeny, and use the hashtag #transformingstigma.

THE STIGMA CYCLE

OVERVIEW

WHEN PEOPLE USE THE TERM "stigma," they aren't referring to the definition; they are referring to the negative impact stigma has on a person, which occurs in a cycle. This is what I call the Stigma Cycle.

1. Stigma starts with shame. According to Oxford Dictionaries, shame is "a painful feeling of humiliation or distress caused by the consciousness of wrong or foolish behavior."

2. Shame leads to silence.

3. Silence leads to sabotage, self-destructive behavior, social injustice, and suicide.

4. The cycle repeats.

Example: Jane has chronic depression (dysthymia). Her boyfriend told her repeatedly to just be tougher and not let things bother her. Jane feels like she can't talk to her boyfriend about her depression, which adds to the shame she feels about her depression. So Jane stops discussing the problem with her partner and decides to be silent about her mental health challenges. She withdraws from her group of friends, takes a week off work, and is eventually fired. As a result, Jane now feels a new sense of shame and needs to find a new source of income.

THE STIGMA CYCLE EXERCISE

In the example above, how could Jane's boyfriend have showed her better support?

_____

_____

_____

_____

_____

_____

_____

Stigma starts with shame. How does the word "shame" make you feel?

_____

_____

_____

_____

_____

What makes you feel shame?

- _____

- _____

- _____

- _____

- _____

How do you deal with shame?

_____

_____

_____

_____

For people with mental health challenges, shame often leads to silence. Why is silence detrimental to someone with a mental health challenge?

_____

_____

_____

_____

_____

_____

How do you think someone trapped in the Stigma Cycle might act differently than someone free from stigma?

_____

_____

_____

_____

How do you believe the Stigma Cycle can be broken?

_____

_____

_____

_____

If the Stigma Cycle is prevented, what issues in society do you think would improve? (Check all that apply.)

☐ Climate change

☐ Terrorism

☐ Poverty

☐ Gun violence

☐ Suicide

☐ Birth rate

☐ Gender inequality

☐ Lack of education

Which of the above do you believe would not improve, and why?

_____

_____

_____

_____

_____

_____

Which from the list above do you believe to be the most important, and why?

_____

_____

_____

_____

How would being free of stigma impact you?

_____

_____

_____

_____

What is one question you still have about stigma?

_____

_____

_____

_____

Before we dive into self-care, I'd love to know what's on your mind at this point. Are you enjoying The Transforming Stigma Workbook? *Take a minute and send me an email at mike@mikeveny.com, and I'll get back to you quickly.*

TRANSFORM SHAME THROUGH SELF-CARE

OVERVIEW

WE OFTEN NEGLECT TAKING CARE of ourselves to handle things we deem to be more urgent (relationships, careers, helping others), and our mental health suffers as a result.

Oxford Dictionaries defines self-care as:

"The practice of taking action to preserve or improve one's own health."

Self-care is an important part of both physical and emotional health. As mentioned in chapter nine of *Transforming Stigma*, self-care activities are different from **escape activities** like watching television, playing video games, substance misuse, or using social media. Self-care activities are intentional and proactive actions that help you grow as a person. I practice self-care by:

- Exercising

- Playing drums

- Attending mental health support group meetings

- Surrounding myself with positive people

- Meditating

- Writing

When I practice self-care, not only do I feel better mentally and physically, but I'm able to give more to others. Visit pages 108–117 of *Transforming Stigma* for more, including how to improve your mornings using Hal Elrod's SAVERS (*The Miracle Morning: The Not-So-Obvious Secret Guaranteed to Transform Your Life Before 8 a.m.*).

SAVERS stands for:

- Silence

- Affirmations

- Visualization

- Exercise

- Reading

- Scribing (Writing)

All of the above are ways to practice self-care.

SELF-CARE EXERCISE

What happens when you don't practice self-care?

_____

_____

_____

_____

How does your commitment to self-care influence other people in your life?

_____

_____

_____

_____

What decisions have you made when hungry, angry, lonely, or tired (HALT) that you have later regretted?

_____

_____

_____

_____

What helps you personally stay/become mentally healthy?

_____

_____

_____

_____

What helps you stay/become physically healthy?

_____

_____

_____

_____

In what ways do your physical and mental well-being overlap?

_____

_____

_____

_____

Could any of the above be considered escape activities—activities you engage in to forget about problems and stresses instead of actively improving your health and well-being? Discuss below.

_____

_____

_____

_____

How do you practice self-care on a regular basis?

_____

_____

_____

_____

List five ways you can practice self-care:

1. _____

2. _____

3. _____

4. _____

5. _____

What gets in the way of practicing self-care?

_____

_____

_____

_____

What do you believe would help someone in your life make the time and commitment to practice self-care?

_____

_____

_____

_____

SCENARIO:

Disclaimer: Decisions regarding medication should be made under the guidance and care of a mental health professional.

Your friend Daniel has recently made the decision to stop taking medication for his mental health challenge. He plans on exercising and eating healthy in order to better control his mental health and to avoid potential side effects and the stigma attached to taking medication. How do you feel about Daniel's plan? What would you tell him as a friend?

_____

_____

_____

_____

If you disagree with Daniel's plan, how do you think you should approach him to discuss your thoughts? What do you think you shouldn't do or say?

_____

_____

_____

_____

What else could you do as a friend to help Daniel successfully practice self-care and improve his mental health?

_____

_____

_____

_____

Mental Wellness Superhero Challenge: Make a commitment to start doing one new self-care activity. After you do it, reflect on your experience below.

_____

_____

_____

_____

TRANSFORM SILENCE THROUGH CONVERSATION

OVERVIEW

Conversation connects us. Despite being told not to talk about my mental challenges as a child, I've found that it can bring people together and break stigma. In fact, it's the key to transforming the deafening silence around the subject of mental health.

"Your feelings are confined to your own mind and you start to feel alone in your mentality."

— *Kassidy Brown*

For me, talking about my mental health openly led to making new friends, finding my therapist, meeting my wife, and learning about myself. Instead of suffering alone with my mental health challenges, I have chosen to share my struggles with others. This lets them know that they are not alone, and it also releases me from the burden of carrying these challenges on my own without help and support.

In *Transforming Stigma*, I compare discussing mental health to breast cancer. Before people felt empowered and comfortable enough to talk about the disease, very little progress was made. Today, billions of dollars are spent on cancer research each year, so those with the disease feel empowered to talk about it and those with it have hope that they will recover. The same can happen with mental health; we just need to start discussing it more.

However, conversations about mental health can be difficult. I recommend following the seven Cs:

- Calmness

Remain calm when discussing mental health. It's a sensitive subject, so whatever you can do to remain calm during the conversation will help you and the others involved have a positive and productive conversation.

- Control

Planning and practicing may not seem like necessary parts of having a conversation, but they are. How you present information and carry yourself in a conversation matters. If I respond with the intricate details of my most recent therapy session when someone asks how I'm doing, it may prevent them from feeling comfortable enough to continue the conversation. Instead, try an honest response without all the intimate details: "I'm having a rough time at home." Depending on the other person's comfort level and interest, this gives them the opportunity to ask deeper questions instead of forcing your information and emotional weight onto them. Exhibit control.

- Consistency

Be consistent with what you say about the topic. For example, I try my best to refer to what others call "mental illness" as "mental health challenges" because that's what I believe is appropriate and what will lead to more effective conversations.

• Compassion

It's hard to know what someone else is going through or what they have experienced until you talk with them. Show compassion during discussions on mental health. It can take a lot of bravery just to join the conversation. Make sure you make them feel welcome, heard, and cared for.

• Confidence

It comes with time and practice, but confidence is important. This is one of the many reasons why having frequent conversations on the topic of mental health is important. Showing confidence in what you're saying will lead to others willingly listening to you. If I mumbled and kept my head down while talking on stage to a group of teenagers, they would quickly tune me out or leave the room.

• Context

I'm the first to admit that finding the right time to start a conversation on mental health is difficult. However, context matters. Find times when it feels right to you to discuss mental health. Remember, the more you do it, the more comfortable you'll feel, and the more opportunities you'll find to talk about it.

• Clarity

Mental health is a confusing subject. Bring clarity to the conversation by defining what mental health means to you. Do your due diligence to understand the latest terminology.

CONVERSATION EXERCISE

List the risks of having a conversation about mental health challenges.

1. _____

2. _____

3. _____

4. _____

5. _____

List each of the risks you presented above and explain what can be done to eliminate or lessen this risk.

Risk #1: _____

How can this risk be lessened or eliminated?

_____

_____

Risk #2: _____

How can this risk be lessened or eliminated?

_____

_____

Risk #3: _____

How can this risk be lessened or eliminated?

_____

_____

Risk #4: _____

How can this risk be lessened or eliminated?

_____

_____

Risk #5: _____

How can this risk be lessened or eliminated?

_____

_____

What benefits can be gained from having conversations about mental health?

- _____
- _____
- _____
- _____
- _____
- _____
- _____

How would you go about starting a conversation about mental health?

_____

_____

_____

_____

Mental Wellness Superhero Challenge: Make a commitment to start a conversation about mental health with one person this week. After the conversation is over, reflect on your experience below.

_____

_____

_____

_____

DISCUSSION TOPICS

Let's keep this conversation going! Remember, there are no right or wrong answers.

- Should those with diagnosed mental health challenges be treated the same as those who do not have mental health challenges when it comes to the following (circle yes or no)?

    o Insurance: Yes   No

Explain: _____

_____

_____

    o Work benefits: Yes   No

Explain: _____

_____

_____

    o Government resources: Yes   No

Explain: _____

_____

_____

o Gun ownership: Yes   No

Explain: _____

_____

_____

o Romantic relationships: Yes   No

Explain: _____

_____

_____

- Should those with mental health challenges be treated differently by the law when facing prosecution for committing a crime? Why or why not? Please explain.

_____

_____

_____

_____

Before we finish the final full section of this workbook, how is it going for you at this point? What is your feedback on the workbook? What questions can I answer for you? Take a minute and send me an email at mike@mikeveny.com, and I'll get back to you quickly.

TRANSFORM SABOTAGE, SOCIAL INJUSTICE, SELF-DESTRUCTIVE BEHAVIOR, AND SUICIDE THROUGH CONNECTION

OVERVIEW

"We are born connected. We feel whole. The second our umbilical cord is cut,
we feel alone. Incomplete. From here on out, we crave connection."

— *John Kim*

CONNECTION IS DEFINED BY MERRIAM-WEBSTER as a "person connected with another especially by marriage, kinship, or common interest." Because mental health is comprised of our thoughts, feelings, and behaviors, relationships play a significant role in the state of our mental health. Strong, positive relationships lead to more positive thoughts, which contribute to feelings, which influence behaviors.

Those whom I share a deep connection with add value to my life. They are individuals whom I can trust, talk to about anything, and contact at any time. They empower me to rise above my own mental health challenges and help others.

The steps outlined in *Transforming Stigma* to help create deep, positive connections include:

- Taking inventory of your relationships

- Constantly educating yourself through

    o Listening

    o Learning

    o Language

- Learning the signs and symptoms of someone who is struggling

- Sharing your story

- Supporting others who are struggling

- Becoming a fierce advocate

CONNECTION EXERCISE

What is needed for a strong connection to form between two people?

_____

_____

_____

_____

_____

Name five people you have a strong connection with:

1. _____

2. _____

3. _____

4. _____

5. _____

What value do strong connections with people bring to your life?

_____

_____

_____

_____

_____

For those with mental health challenges but without strong connections with others, what would you recommend for them to find and establish those relationships?

_____

_____

_____

_____

_____

What separates a positive connection from one that is harmful to a person and their mental health?

_____

_____

_____

_____

How do you go about limiting the damage a negative relationship is having on your life?

_____

_____

_____

_____

Why is learning the signs and symptoms of someone who is struggling important? What would you do once you recognize those signs in someone?

_____

_____

_____

_____

Education is important. How can you educate yourself about mental health challenges?

_____

_____

_____

_____

What steps are you going to take today to become an advocate for those with mental health challenges?

_____

_____

_____

_____

Are you comfortable sharing your story and your struggles with your mental health? Why or why not? If you're not, what would make you feel comfortable sharing?

_____

_____

_____

_____

If you feel comfortable sharing below, outline how you would share your mental health story with someone.

For tips on sharing your story, I recommend reading *Challenging the Stigma of Mental Illness* by Corrigan, Roe, and Tsang, or reading the tips outlined on pages 150–151 of *Transforming Stigma*.

_____

_____

_____

_____

Mental Wellness Superhero Challenge: Make a commitment to share your story with a person or group who has never heard your story. After you share it, reflect on your experience below.

_____

_____

_____

_____

CONCLUSION

Whether it's you who is struggling, someone you love, or someone you don't know, mental health challenges are confusing and frustrating. We need superheroes in this ongoing fight. This fight is for our own health, for the lives of our friends, families, and neighbors around the world, and for the betterment of the universe. Be proud you took a step toward transforming the stigma surrounding mental health.

CONCLUDING EXERCISE

How are you feeling, superhero? I mean really, how are you feeling? Please take a few minutes to reflect on how this workbook has made you feel and what you have learned about yourself.

_____

_____

_____

_____

_____

_____

_____

_____

Before leaving this workbook, I want to encourage you to keep exploring, be curious, and ask questions. I thank you for taking this journey with me, and I believe that after finishing this journey, you are now better prepared to improve and save lives—maybe even yours or mine.

Continue your journey, superhero, and I hope that our paths cross again.

Sincerely,

Mike Veny

PS. If you have enjoyed and gained value from this workbook, could you take a minute to leave a review on your favorite retailer? Your review will help others find this workbook. Thank you in advance for furthering the conversation on mental health!

APPENDIX 1: MENTAL HEALTH
HELP HOTLINES & WEBSITES

T HESE RESOURCES COULD HELP YOU either find the help you need or the information you are looking for. While I have not personally used every one of these resources and am not endorsing any of them (it's up to you to determine which ones will benefit you), I do urge you to reach out to one of these resources if you are struggling.

CRISIS / SUICIDE PREVENTION

The National Suicide Prevention Lifeline

The National Suicide Prevention Lifeline is a free service that can be used by anyone experiencing suicidal thoughts, family members who are concerned about a loved one, and professionals who are looking for additional resources. You can speak with someone over the phone and they can put you in contact with a local center. This is available 24/7, so someone will be there whenever you need them.

Phone: 1-800-273-TALK (8255)

Website: http://suicidepreventionlifeline.org

The American Foundation for Suicide Prevention

The American Foundation for Suicide Prevention works to fund scientific research and raise awareness for those who are struggling with or affected by suicide. They provide resources for support groups and professionals as well as to individuals struggling with suicidal thoughts.

Phone: 1-888-333-2377

Website: https://afsp.org

HopeLine

HopeLine, made up of independent volunteers, is a confidential telephone service for people who are in crisis. Since their volunteers are not professional counselors, if they feel that your situation is outside of what they are able to assist with, they will connect you to the appropriate source.

Phone: 1-877-235-4525 (call or text)

Website: https://www.hopeline-nc.org

Crisis Text Line

Crisis Text Line is a free hotline that has counselors available 24/7 to help anyone in a crisis. If you aren't comfortable talking to someone, texting can be a good option for getting the help you need.

Text the word CONNECT to 741741

IMALIVE

IMALIVE is an online chat-based resource run by the Kristin Brooks Hope Center. Additionally, they run programs for high schools and colleges. If you are experiencing a crisis, have suicidal thoughts, or are dealing with intense emotional pain, the volunteers on their chat line can help.

Website: https://www.imalive.org

GAMBLING

National Council on Problem Gambling

The National Council on Problem Gambling offers several ways for family members of addicts and those addicted to gambling to get help. They provide literature on treatment and recovery options and the hotline can help you get connected with local resources.

Phone: 1-800-522-4700

Chat: www.ncpagambling.org/chat

Online peer support forum: www.gamtalk.org

Website: https://www.ncpagambling.org

GRIEF

Compassionate Friends

Compassionate Friends provides help for family members after the death of a child. They offer support through local chapters and online communities. There is a wealth of knowledge on their website, and you can request a bereavement packet that can be customized to your situation. Through their website, you can find the closest chapter to you from their list of over six hundred chapters.

Phone: 1-630-990-0010

Website: https://www.compassionatefriends.org

LGBTQ SUPPORT

LGBT National Hotline

The LGBT National Help Center works to assist people who have questions about gender identity and sexual orientation. They run three hotlines and offer private one-on-one online chats. They can help with issues like coming out, safer sex, school bullying, relationship problems, and family concerns. They also have online chat rooms for youth and teens to help them find a community of acceptance.

Phone: 1-888-843-4564

LGBT National Youth Talkline: 1-800-246-7743

LGBT National Senior Talkline: 1-888-234-7243

Email: help@LGBThotline.org

Website: https://www.glbthotline.org

MENTAL HEALTH

National Alliance on Mental Illness (NAMI)

NAMI does not provide counseling; however, they do provide information about mental health issues such as symptoms and treatment options. They can also help connect you with support groups. You can reach out to the national office to be connected with your state chapter, or you can find out more information on their website.

Phone: 1-800-950-6264

Website: http://www.nami.org

Anxiety and Depression Association of America (ADAA)

The ADAA provides access to information to help in the prevention and treatment of anxiety and depression. Their website is full of information, and they do have an option to find a local therapist.

Phone: 1-240-485-1001

Website: https://adaa.org

Children and Adults with Attention-Deficit / Hyperactivity Disorder (CHADD)

The CHADD website has information for professionals, educators, parents, and adults who are living with ADHD. You can reach a specialist on the phone from 1 p.m. to 5 p.m. EST Monday through Friday.

Phone: 1-800-233-4050

Website: https://chadd.org

International OCD Foundation

The International OCD Foundation has resources and information to help you learn more about OCD. They can also help connect you with trained professionals within your local area.

Phone: 1-617-973-5801

Website: https://iocdf.org

Treatment and Research Advancements for Borderline Personality Disorder (TARA)

TARA provides access to researched-based information and helps individuals cope with borderline personality disorder. Whether you are the one struggling or it's one of your loved ones, they can connect you with local resources for treatment and support.

Phone: 1-888-482-7227

Website: www.tara4bpd.org

SUBSTANCE ABUSE

Substance Abuse and Mental Health Services Administration (SAMHSA)

SAMHSA's mission is to "reduce the impact of substance abuse and mental illness on America's communities." This agency is part of the US Department of Health and Human Services. They provide information that can help you locate treatment options within your area. The office is open Monday through Friday from 8 a.m. to 8 p.m. EST.

Phone: 1-877-SAMHSA7 (1-877-726-4727)

Website: https://www.samhsa.gov

National Council on Alcoholism and Drug Dependence (NCADD)

NCADD works to connect individuals to the right resources in their community to help them recover from addiction. When you call the number below, you will be redirected to a local center based on the zip code you enter.

Phone: 1-800-622-2255

Website: https://www.ncadd.org

TEEN HEALTH

Partnership for Drug-Free Kids

This free hotline provides one-on-one help for parents, family members, or caregivers who are looking for help with a child's substance abuse. The phones are answered by trained specialists Monday through Friday from 9 a.m. to midnight EST and Saturday and Sunday from 12 p.m. through 5 p.m. EST.

Phone: 1-855-378-4373

Text: 55753

Website: https://drugfree.org (you can also email a specialist from a form on the website)

Trevor HelpLine

The Trevor Project works to provide suicide intervention and crisis intervention for LGBTQ individuals who are under the age of twenty-five. The hotline is available 24/7; the online chat and text options are available every day from noon through 1 a.m. EST.

Phone: 1-866-488-7386

Text the word START to 678678

Website: https://www.thetrevorproject.org

Teen Line

Teen Line provides teen-to-teen support from 9 p.m. to 1 a.m. EST for teenagers who are struggling and want to talk to another teen who knows what they're talking about. They also provide resources, information, and message boards.

Phone: 1-800-852-8336

Text the word TEEN to 839863

Veterans Crisis Line

The Veterans Crisis Line is there 24/7 to support any veterans, service members, National Guard and Reserve members or their family and friends who are experiencing a crisis. You can contact qualified responders from the Department of Veterans Affairs by calling, texting, or using an online chat.

Phone: 1-800-273-8255

Text: 838255

Chat: connect on their website https://www.veteranscrisisline.net

APPENDIX 2: HOW TO USE A MENTAL HEALTH HOTLINE

I f you or a loved one is struggling with mental health, know that you are not alone. You are not the only person to feel like you do, and there are people who care about you and want to help. If you don't know whom to turn to, there are plenty of hotlines you can call. The people who answer these calls are there because you are important, and they want to assist you in getting help.

If you think there is any chance that you or someone else you know might harm yourself or others, contact 911 immediately.

But if you simply don't know where to turn to get help for yourself or someone else, or if you don't know if you even should call someone, I urge you to reach out to one of the numbers listed in Appendix 1.

WHO SHOULD CALL

Anyone can call a mental health hotline. The people on the other end of the phone are trained to speak to people suffering from mental health challenges, family members that do not know what to do next, and people who just have questions in general.

Do not feel that your situation is not "bad enough" or a "big enough deal" to warrant calling a hotline. These hotlines are here to serve people whether or not you have a simple question or need to find professional help.

WHAT TO EXPECT FROM YOUR CALL

I know that it can be intimidating and maybe even a little scary to pick up a phone and make the call. But there's no reason to be afraid. While each hotline is slightly different, you can expect the following:

- At first, you will hear a recorded message. It may include things like what button to push based on your language.

- The recording will tell you if you're going to be routed to a local center, and then you will hold while someone is placed on your call.

- A trained counselor will answer your call. Many hotlines don't require you to provide your name if you aren't comfortable doing so.

- The call is entirely about you and to help you. The counselor may ask you some questions about your situation if you are having a difficult time communicating why you called. They will listen to you. They will also provide resources that will benefit you specifically.

Remember, you are in complete control of the call. The person is simply there to help you. They can be a listening ear, connect you with a mental health professional, or provide you with options of next steps you could take. The calls are confidential unless you specify that you would like them to share the information, or if they believe you are a danger to yourself or someone else.

APPENDIX 3: MENTAL HEALTH MYTHS VS. FACTS

THERE ARE A LOT OF myths surrounding mental health. These myths are a large part of what builds the mental health stigma. Believing these myths causes one to act and treat someone with mental health challenges a certain way. But that's not all: many people struggling with their own mental health believe these myths. That's part of what keeps them unable to move forward toward recovery.

I encourage you to read through this next section with an open mind. Use the information and links provided to challenge and change the myths that you've been believing:

MYTH: PEOPLE DIAGNOSED WITH MENTAL HEALTH DISORDERS ARE MORE DANGEROUS.

This myth is commonly found in the media, especially after tragic events like mass shootings. The common belief is that people with mental challenges, especially those diagnosed with schizophrenia and bipolar disorder, are more likely to commit a crime.

Fact: People diagnosed with mental challenges are actually more likely to be the victim of a crime than to commit a crime themselves. When there are tragic events such as mass shootings, people are quick to throw mental health into the conversation. However, the American Mental Health Counselors Association has stated that including incidents with firearms, mental health is behind only three to five percent of all violent crimes.

Source for more information: www.mentalhealthamerica.net/positions/violence and www.amhca.org

Tip: Share your story! If more people who struggle with mental health were willing to share their stories, society would become familiar with the truth about mental health challenges. If you struggle yourself, don't be afraid to share your experience with others. It will help everyone in the end.

MYTH: PEOPLE WITH MENTAL HEALTH CHALLENGES AREN'T ABLE TO FUNCTION IN SOCIETY.

Fact: One in four people will be impacted by a mental health challenge at some point in their life. There are many levels of mental health challenges, from anxiety and depression to schizophrenia and psychosis. The truth is, you are crossing paths and interacting with people every day who are "mentally ill"; you just don't realize it. While there are some instances where those struggling with mental health challenges are unable to function in society on their own, that's the exception and not the rule.

Source for more information: www.who.int/whr/2001/media_centre/press_release/en/

Tip: If you are struggling with your mental health to the point that you are struggling to function in your daily life, you need to seek professional help. There are many forms of treatment for mental health, and there's a good chance that finding the right combination of treatment options will help restore your daily life function.

MYTH: MENTAL HEALTH IS NOT A PROBLEM FOR CHILDREN.

Fact: Adults aren't the only ones who experience mental health challenges. One in five children will suffer from challenges with their mental health. This myth is incredibly dangerous to the mental health of children because many statistics show that early detection is a very important part of recovery. The sooner the child is treated, the less likely their chance of developing serious problems with their mental health. However, only a third of children are receiving the treatment they need at this time.

Source for more information: www.mentalhealthamerica.net/positions/early-identification

Tip: If you have a child who seems like they could be struggling, do not delay in taking them to see a professional. If they get the help they need now, it could stop them from experiencing further challenges in the future.

MYTH: IF SOMEONE WANTS TO STOP STRUGGLING WITH THEIR MENTAL HEALTH, ALL THEY HAVE TO DO IS CHOOSE TO STOP.

Fact: Mental health challenges are real health conditions. They can be caused by genetics, brain chemistry, and exposure to environmental stressors prior to birth. Just because you can't physically see what other people are experiencing does not mean it's not real. People are not choosing to have these challenges in their life. For example, someone who is diagnosed with depression can't simply decide that they are going to "feel better" and "be happy." This can be difficult for people to understand if they haven't experienced it themselves.

Source for more information:
www.mentalhealthamerica.net/recognizing-warning-signs

and www.mayoclinic.org/diseases-conditions/mental-illness/symptoms-causes/syc-20374968

Tip: If you've never experienced mental health challenges personally, you're doing the right thing by reading this book. Continue to educate yourself on the topic to increase your understanding, and don't pass judgment on those who are struggling. Ask them to explain their experience to you.

If you have mental health challenges and are being judged by others, stand up for yourself. Some people won't understand no matter how hard you try to educate them. When that happens, you might need to distance yourself from them if they continue to give you a hard time. Talk to a therapist for support.

MYTH: THERE'S NO REAL RECOVERY FROM MENTAL HEALTH CHALLENGES. ONCE YOU HAVE IT, YOU HAVE TO DEAL WITH IT FOR LIFE.

Fact: Mental health challenges are treatable. There are also instances where people only experience symptoms from a mental health challenge for a brief period of time in their life. Just because someone has received a diagnosis does not necessarily mean it's something that they will always deal with. And there are many forms of treatment available to help individuals work toward recovery while improving their quality of life.

Source for more information: www.mentalhealthamerica.net/recovery-support

Tip: If you are struggling with your mental health, don't lose hope. There are many options available for treatment based on the specific challenges you are facing. Make an appointment and get help from a licensed mental health professional. With trial and error, you will be able to discover a treatment plan that works for you.

MYTH: MEDICATION IS THE ONLY FORM OF TREATMENT.

Fact: There are many different options for treatment. Licensed therapists have a vast number of therapies they can use when treating you. There are also options such as support groups, psychiatric service dogs, meditation, self-care, and more. For some people, medication will be a part of their treatment plan. However, some people will be able to create a treatment plan without the need for a prescription.

Source for more information:
www.psychiatry.org/patients-families/what-is-mental-illness
and www.mentalhealthamerica.net/types-mental-health-treatments

Tip: If you are treating your mental health challenges only with medication, I encourage you to try including other forms of therapy as well. It could allow you to reduce the medication you are taking or eliminate it altogether. However, there is no shame in using medication to help you with your mental health challenges. Find the treatment that works best for you.

MYTH: THERE'S NOTHING I CAN DO TO HELP SOMEONE WITH MENTAL HEALTH CHALLENGES.

Fact: Many people believe that because they are not professionals, there's nothing they can do to help those with mental health challenges. And it might be true that you can't provide them with therapy, but the truth is, that's not what they need from you. Hurting and struggling people need support. They need to know they aren't being judged and there are people supporting them. They may not even reach out to talk to you about it, but just knowing that you are there if they want to talk can make all the difference.

Source for more information: You're holding it in your hands right now.

Tip: Look back through this book and pick one actionable thing to do. If you know someone who is struggling, reach out to them. If you don't personally know of anyone, then look for ways to fight the stigma in your community.

APPENDIX 4: SUGGESTED READING LIST

THE DEPRESSION CURE: THE 6-STEP PROGRAM TO BEAT DEPRESSION WITHOUT DRUGS

In this book, author Stephen Ilardi shares a six-step program based on his proven Therapeutic Lifestyle Change program. He theorizes that we are seeing such high levels of depression in society today because our bodies were not designed to handle the current way that most of us live. His six steps take you back to the way people used to survive, and the way some cultures, like aboriginal groups, still do. This includes the following components:

- Brain Food

- Don't Think, Do

- Antidepressant Exercise (using exercise as an antidepressant)

- Let There Be Light (spending time in the sun, soaking up vitamin D)

- Get Connected

- Habits of Healthy Sleep

If you are looking for alternative or supplemental treatment ideas for depression, this book is for you.

THE BODY KEEPS THE SCORE: BRAIN, MIND, AND BODY IN THE HEALING OF TRAUMA

In this book, author Dr. Bessel van der Kolk explains the physical impact that trauma (all forms, like physical, sexual, and emotional abuse) has on our brain.

Dr. van der Kolk explains that trauma can actually rewire the way our brain works. This makes an impact on our levels of control, engagement, trust, and pleasure. He also shares what we can do that will help us undo the damage including mindfulness, yoga, and other therapies.

ANY BOOK BY STEPHEN HINSHAW

Stephen Hinshaw has written multiple books that are helpful resources on mental health. He has a long list of accomplishments in the field of mental health, including being a professor of psychology at both UC San Francisco and UC Berkeley and has been recognized by groups across the country.

- *ADHD: What Everyone Needs to Know*

- *The Mark of Shame: Signs of Mental Illness and Agenda for Change*

- *Breaking the Silence: Mental Health Professionals Disclose Their Personal and Family Experiences with Mental Illness*

- *The Triple Bind: Saving Our Teenage Girls from Today's Pressures and Conflicting Expectations*

- *Origins of the Human Mind*

- *The ADHD Explosion: Myths, Medication, Money, and Today's Push for Performance*

- *Another Kind of Madness: A Journey Through the Stigma and Hope of Mental Illness*

ANY BOOKS BY PATRICK CORRIGAN

Patrick Corrigan is a professor of psychology at the Illinois Institute of Technology. He has held many other prestigious positions and has devoted decades to helping patients with psychiatric disabilities and their families. This past decade he has largely focused on addressing the stigma surrounding mental health.

- *Challenging the Stigma of Mental Illness: Lessons for Therapists and Advocates* (written with David Roe and Hector W. H. Tsang)

- *Don't Call Me Nuts: Coping with the Stigma of Mental Illness* (written with Robert Lundin)

- *The Stigma of Disease and Disability: Understanding Causes and Overcoming Injustices*

- *Coming Out Proud to Erase the Stigma of Mental Illness: Stories and Essays of Solidarity* (written with Jon E. Larson and Patrick J. Michaels)

- *Recovery in Mental Illness: Broadening Our Understanding of Wellness* (written with Ruth O. Ralph)

I HATE YOU—DON'T LEAVE ME: UNDERSTANDING THE BORDERLINE PERSONALITY

For more than two decades, this book by Jerold Kreisman has been considered the guide to BPD. It dives into the disorder along with its connection to other mental health disorders. There is a revised and updated book on the market. If you are looking to understand your BPD or just want a better understanding of the disorder, this is a great book to check out.

ANXIETY SUCKS! A TEEN SURVIVAL GUIDE

This book by Natasha Daniels is a great read for teens and adults. It breaks down what anxiety looks and sounds like in our lives, providing practical examples that preteens and teens can relate to and easy-to-follow steps they can take in order to overcome it.

CHANGE YOUR BRAIN, CHANGE YOUR LIFE: THE BREAKTHROUGH PROGRAM FOR CONQUERING ANXIETY, DEPRESSION, OBSESSIVENESS, ANGER, AND IMPULSIVENESS

In this book, author Daniel Amen goes into detail about how your brain works and what you can do to pinpoint your problems along with what you can do in order to address each area and improve functionality. It includes options like nutrition, medication, and cognitive exercises. If you are easily controlled by your emotions and experience anxiety and depression, this is a good read.

BOOK MIKE VENY TO SPEAK

What do you get when you mix mental health challenges with a passion for drumming? A dynamic speaker and musician who delivers raw energy with a fresh perspective on wellness!

Mike Veny is a highly sought-after keynote mental health speaker, corporate drumming event facilitator, author, and luggage enthusiast. Seriously, you'd completely get it if you did all the traveling he did! He's the author of the book *Transforming Stigma: How to Become a Mental Wellness Superhero*. As a 2017 PM360 ELITE Award Winner, Mike is recognized as one of the 100 most influential people in the healthcare industry.

He loves working with leaders who are tired of bringing the same old textbook presentations to their events. If you are looking for a proven speaker who will connect with, entertain, and engage your audience—all while educating and uniting them around improving wellness—you've come to the right place.

You can feel confident having Mike as your keynote speaker or workshop facilitator. Over the years, his expertise has been honored with remarkable and notable accolades. He has served on the board of directors of the Fender Music Foundation and the Rotary Club of Wall Street New York; he is an ambassador for Self-Employment in the Arts and was a presenter at the Haiti Entrepreneurship Camp.

Mike's path to becoming a public speaker became evident at an early age. **He convinced the staff at psychiatric hospitals to discharge him three times during his childhood.** In addition to being hospitalized as a child, he was expelled from three schools, attempted suicide, and was medicated in efforts to reduce his emotional instability and behavioral outbursts.

By the fifth grade, Mike was put in a special education class. Aside from getting more individualized attention from the teacher, he learned that pencil erasers make a great sound when tapped on a desk. *He had no idea that drumming would become his career or his path to recovery.*

As an adult, Mike spent many years facilitating drum workshops for children with special needs, teaching them to channel their energy by banging a drum and at the same time learning how to listen, focus, work together and succeed through teamwork. The project was such a hit that he continued to expand his drumming program, first to adults in recovery and eventually into the corporate setting.

Whether the focus of your event is leadership, motivation, or suicide prevention, Mike draws on his personal and painful experiences to deliver keynotes, presentations, and workshops that take your event to the next level.

With more than fifteen years of experience making meeting planners look good, Mike is committed to:

- Providing an abundance of helpful information to audiences

- Creating innovative drumming workshops to empower teamwork

- Delivering epic live events that inspire action

Mike's perspectives have been featured on ABC, NBC, and CBS News. He was a former guest on the *Fresh Outlook* TV news show, a writer for *Corporate Wellness Magazine* and HealthCentral.com. "Mental Illness is An Asset", his compelling TEDx talk, has been used in college classrooms and gotten sensational reviews.

Mike's authenticity, straightforward approach, and easy-to-understand takeaways set him apart from other speakers. The audience will walk away with knowledge that they can put to use immediately in their own lives, with their loved ones, or in the workplace.

It's that simple!

Mike's vision for events aligns with your vision—**hold a powerful and unforgettable experience that provides real value to your meeting attendees.**

Want to get to know Mike a little more?

- He doesn't use PowerPoint or speak with notes in his presentations. (Hint: That's where all that authenticity comes from.)

- He's a member of the Rotary Club of Wall Street. Being a Rotarian has contributed to his happiness.

- He loves to travel and is obsessed with luggage, packing techniques, and travel checklists.

- He takes his morning routine very seriously.

- He enjoys a really good bone-in rib eye steak cooked medium rare.

Connect with Mike today and explore how he can add value to your upcoming event and give your audience the memory of a lifetime. Visit www.mikeveny.com/contact.

ACKNOWLEDGMENTS

THE COMPLETION OF MY SECOND book could have not been made possible without the participation, support, and help from a long list of people. I appreciate all of their efforts and am grateful for their contributions. However, I would like to express sincere appreciation and indebtedness mainly to the following:

I am thankful to Michael Luchies and his gifts as a writer. None of this would have been possible without him. His attention to detail and willingness to disagree with me is what got this book finished.

Special thanks to Kate Tilton for her expert guidance on publishing. She is constantly teaching me and challenging me to get better at publishing books, and most importantly, publish a piece of art.

I place on record my sincerest thanks to my mentor, Michael Hartstein. His feedback helped me understand the need for writing a second book and making it a workbook.

And most importantly, I'd like to thank my wife, Denelle. She is my best friend and biggest fan. I am grateful for her unconditional love, her belief in me and her unwavering support of me.

ABOUT THE AUTHOR

Mike Veny (pronounced *"Vee-Knee"*) is a highly sought-after keynote mental health speaker, corporate drumming event facilitator, author, and luggage enthusiast. Seriously, you'd completely get it if you did all the traveling he did! As a 2017 PM360 ELITE Award Winner, Mike is recognized as one of the 100 most influential people in the healthcare industry.

At an early age, Mike convinced the staff at psychiatric hospitals to discharge him three times during his childhood. In addition to being hospitalized as a child, he was expelled from three schools, attempted suicide, and was medicated in efforts to reduce his emotional instability and behavioral outbursts.

By the fifth grade, Mike was put in a special education class. Aside from getting more individualized attention from the teacher, he learned that pencil erasers make a great sound when tapped on a desk. He had no idea that drumming would become his career or his path to recovery.

As an adult, Mike spent many years facilitating drum workshops for children with special needs, teaching them to channel their energy by banging a drum and at the same time learning how to listen, focus, work together and succeed through teamwork. The project was such a hit that he continued to expand his drumming program, first to adults in recovery and eventually into the corporate setting.

Visit Mike online at www.mikeveny.com.

Made in the USA
Middletown, DE
17 July 2021